# MAMMALS

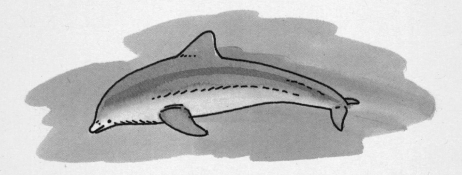

**Troll Associates**

# MAMMALS

by Francene Sabin

Illustrated by Joseph Veno

**Troll Associates**

*Library of Congress Cataloging in Publication Data*

Sabin, Francene.
  Mammals.

    Summary: An introduction to the large group of ani-
mals which grows hair, produces milk for their babies,
and gives birth to living young.
    1. Mammals—Juvenile literature.  [1. Mammals]
I. Veno, Joseph, ill.  II. Title.
QL706.2.S23     1984         599        84-2658
ISBN 0-8167-0208-X (lib. bdg.)
ISBN 0-8167-0209-8 (pbk.)

Mice, bats, whales, dogs, monkeys, and human beings look very different. But they all have something in common. Every one of them is a mammal. In fact, there are between four thousand and five thousand different species of mammals on Earth.

Some are enormous, like the blue whale. If a blue whale could stand on its tail, it would be as tall as a ten-story building. But most mammals are not nearly that big. Some are tiny, like the shrew, which is about the length of your little finger.

The bat is a mammal that flies. The flying squirrel is a mammal that glides through the air, from tree to tree. The porcupine is a mammal with sharp quills that protect it from enemies. Another mammal—the armadillo—is covered by hard plates that protect it like armor. The sea lion, the walrus, and the seal are mammals that live in the ocean and on the shore. And mammals like the mouse, the mole, and the chipmunk live in underground nests.

Mammals come in many sizes, shapes, and colors, but they are all alike in certain ways. First of all, every mammal is a vertebrate. That means it has a skeleton with a backbone. And every mammal has lungs it uses to breathe air. Mammals are also warm-blooded animals. Whether the temperature around it is hot or cold, a mammal's body temperature stays just about the same.

Of all the creatures on Earth, only mammals can grow hair. Only mammals produce milk to feed their young. And except for the platypus and the spiny anteater, all mammals give birth to living young.

Perhaps more important than anything else is the fact that the brains of mammals are more highly developed than the brains of birds or fish or reptiles or insects. That makes mammals more intelligent. And of all the mammals, human beings are the most intelligent. We are the only species with a spoken and written language.

We are also the only species able to create machines and change the environment around us. After human beings, the most intelligent mammals are chimpanzees, gorillas, dolphins, and porpoises.

Human beings, monkeys, and chimpanzees all belong to the same large order, or group, of mammals. This is called the primate order.

Dogs, cats, bears, and lions belong to a different order. They are carnivores, or meat-eating mammals. Another order contains the rodents, such as rats, mice, squirrels, and beavers, who have chisel-shaped teeth that are good for gnawing.

And still another order contains the marsupials, including such animals as kangaroos and opossums.

Like all other mammals, marsupials give birth to living young—the babies do not hatch from eggs. But marsupial babies are not yet fully developed when they are born. Even the babies of large marsupials, like kangaroos, are less than an inch long at birth. They are deaf, blind, and hairless. They crawl into a pouch on their mother's body, where they will remain until they are ready to take care of themselves.

Besides the marsupials, rodents, carnivores, and primates, there are many other groups of mammals. Altogether, there are eighteen different orders!

All but one of the mammals that live on land move around on four limbs. Human beings are the only mammals that stand, walk, and run on two legs all the time. This leaves the front limbs, called arms, free to carry things. Other primates, such as the chimpanzee, sometimes move on two limbs, but not all the time.

Horses and deer are mammals with hard hooves to protect their feet. Their hooves make it possible for them to run well over almost every kind of ground. Cats, dogs, and wolves walk on their toes, which are leathery pads. These pads allow them to move very quietly.

Many tree-living mammals have sharp, curved claws. Other tree-dwellers have tails that they use almost like hands. The spider monkey will hold onto a tree branch with its tail while using its four feet to hold and peel a piece of fruit.

Mammals are adapted to their environments in a variety of ways. The flying squirrel has a thin membrane of skin stretched between the front and rear legs. When the squirrel leaps from tree to tree, the membranes act like a sail or parachute. The bat, however, is the only true flying mammal, and the only one with real wings.

Mammals that live in watery environments must be adapted to swimming. The beaver has a broad, flat tail that acts as a rudder as it moves through the water. Seals and walruses are swift, graceful swimmers but are quite clumsy on land. Their limbs, which are short flippers, are wonderful for swimming, but not much use for walking.

Whales and dolphins are among the mammals that spend all their lives in the water. Over millions of years, their rear limbs have disappeared completely. These mammals have streamlined bodies, small flippers—which are all that remain of their front legs—and a powerful tail. In many ways, these mammals seem like fish.

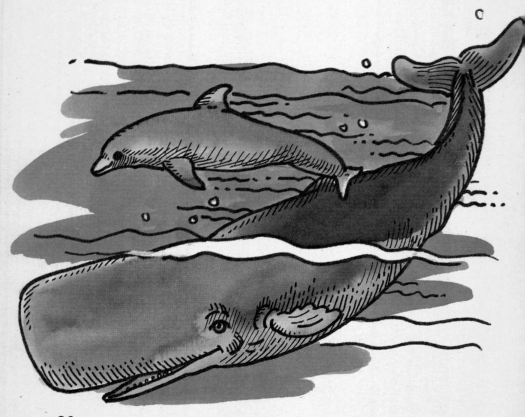

However, unlike fish, they must come to the surface to breathe air, and they give birth to live young, instead of laying eggs like fish do.

Many of the mammals that live in and near the ocean eat fish and shellfish. They have sharp, backward-pointing teeth to help them catch and hold on to their slippery prey. Meat-eating mammals that live on land have sharp teeth designed for tearing and chewing.

Grazing animals, or mammals that eat grass and other plants, have broad back teeth that enable them to grind their food. Among the grazing animals are sheep, cattle, and horses.

A rodent's teeth might wear away on its diet of hard-shelled nuts and seeds, except for an interesting fact. A rodent's two front biting teeth keep growing all its life. So as its teeth are wearing down, they are also growing back again.

Some mammals have very special food preferences. The anteater tears open an ant or termite nest with its clawed feet. Then it sticks its long snout into the open nest and collects its food with its long, sticky tongue. The koala, an Australian marsupial that looks like a teddy bear, eats mostly the leaves of the eucalyptus tree.

The majority of mammals are plant-eaters, or herbivores. In tropical parts of the world, where plants thrive all year, the animals that eat them have no trouble finding food. But in many other parts of the world, winter reduces the supply of plant food for the herbivores. Some animals solve the problem by storing food to eat during the winter. Chipmunks, squirrels, and many kinds of mice do this.

Some animals, such as the rabbit deer, do not store food. They eat grasses and leaves when these are available, and tree bark and berries in the cold months. And some animals migrate to warmer climates as the weather turns colder. The caribou is a reindeer that lives in northern Canada and Alaska. When winter comes, huge herds of caribou travel from the far north to where they can find food.

There are mammals that solve the problem of winter by going into a special kind of deep sleep known as hibernation. Gophers and woodchucks, or ground hogs, are examples of animals that hibernate when winter comes. A hibernating animal's body temperature drops very low, its breathing slows down, and its heart beats much slower than normal.

Bears may go to sleep for much of the long, cold winter, but they do not really hibernate. Their temperature, heartbeat, and rate of breathing do not change.

Bears usually make their homes in caves or rocky dens. Other mammals, including bats, also live in caves or cavelike places. Many others make their homes in holes in trees or in rocky hollows.

Still other mammals, such as rodents, usually build their homes in underground tunnels. They make a snug nest with grass and twigs. Here the young are born and cared for until they are ready to go out on their own.

Beavers build lodges in the water. The lodges are made of tree branches, mud, and stones. The beavers go in and out through an underwater passage, but their living quarters are above the water line.

When a beaver is threatened, it smacks its tail on the water to warn other beavers of danger. Then it dives deep underwater, where it can hide for as long as fifteen minutes.

Hiding is also the main defense of many other mammals. Some rabbits, for example, have camouflage, or protective coloration, that helps them to hide. Their coats are brown, or spotted with brown, in the summer, so they can blend with the plant life around them. Then their coats turn white in winter, so they are hard to see against the snow.

The hard-shelled armadillo curls into a ball as its defense, while the porcupine's quills defend it against many enemies. And, of course, the skunk's smell is a very well-known defensive weapon!

It's amazing that animals as different as skunks and squirrels, porcupines and porpoises, cats and bats, and kangaroos and walruses can have something in common. Yet they do. They all have backbones. They all have lungs and breathe air. They are all warm-blooded animals with hair somewhere on their bodies. Except for the platypus and the spiny anteater, they all give birth to living young. And they all feed their babies with mother's milk.

They all share these characteristics because they are all members of the same large group of animals—the mammals.